# VISITATIONS

VISITATIONS

৶

POEMS

৶

ADRÉ MARSHALL

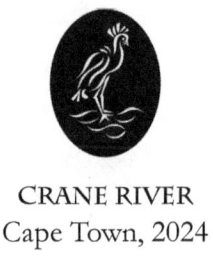

CRANE RIVER
Cape Town, 2024

ACKNOWLEDGEMENTS
....

Some of the poems here collected first appeared in *Carapace*, *New Contrast*, *English Academy Review* and *Stanzas*, on the AVBOB Poetry Competition website and in the AVBOB Poetry Competition anthologies, *I Wish I'd Said...* Vol. 4 and Vol. 6.
'Autumnal' won 3rd prize in the 2022 AVBOB Poetry Competition.

ISBN 978-0-7961-5615-0
© This compilation, Crane River 2024
© Individual poems, Adré Marshall 2024

All rights reserved. No part of this publication may be reproduced, stored in a retrieval system, or transmitted by any form whatsoever without the prior permission of the author or the publisher.

Editor & Publisher: Crane River
Layout and typesetting: User Friendly
Typeset in Garamond 11.5 on 14 pt
Distribution: uHlanga
Proofed by: Danya Ristić-Schacherl
Cover art: Robert Brooks (1941–2024), *Eastern Cape View*
Author photograph: Crane River

CONTENTS

Cederberg Visitation	9
Lachenalias	10
Nightjar	11
From Chipinda Pools	12
Lost	14
Gleaning	15
Beachings	17
At the Waterhole	19
The Fishermen on Fish Hoek Beach	20
Candelabra Lilies	21
Sugarbush	22
On Noordhoek Peak	23
Absence	24
Locks	25
Chartres Revisited	26
Chameleon	27
The Way Out	29
Birthing	30
Out of Sync	31
Courting	32
Cancer Bush	33
Corona Paranoia	34
Walking between Walls	35
Mona Lisa	36
Assisted Living	37
The Last Stretch	38
Lagoon	39
The Hive	40
Down, Not Out	41
Courgettes	42
In Dire Need	43

Descending a Staircase	44
Hospital Visit	45
Visiting Hour	46
Carpe	47
Packing Up	48
Eclipse	49
October Lilies	50
Grave Matters	51
Paternoster	52
Childhood	53
Gnarling	54
A Letter to Stalin's Daughter	55
Doll's House	57
Ginkgo	59
When Does Time Bring Relief?	60
The Purple Season	61
After	63
Spotted Eagle Owls	64
Autumnal	65
Message	66
The Last Supper	67
Biographical note	68

for Rod

(1940–2023)

Cederberg Visitation

After a long day's hike,
we flopped down around the fire
in a loose orbit, five separate worlds
around a bowl of flames.

One nursed a blister, another a grudge
that had festered daylong on the stony slopes,
blurring the beauty of the sculpted rocks
and tawny restios rippling in the breeze's palm.

Some sat with cold fingers outstretched
to the lapping flames, some with hands locked,
faces closed, while over our heads, stars
seethed and whirled in the slatey sky.

From behind the rocks a long shadow
flowed out and snaked its way towards
our fire, eyes glinting as it probed,
sharp-muzzled, among the stones.

We all sat rooted, holding our breath
as the wisp of darkness became a blurred
pelt of stripes and spots gliding around the fire
and past our frozen forms, before floating away.

Someone stirred and a voice rasped,
"Genet." High above our silent heads,
numberless galaxies sparked and swarmed
in the ancient matrix of the sky.

Lachenalias

All those years ago, we rescued bulbs
spurfowl had scratched out of their shelter
between granite rocks. The mauve flowers
wilted, but when transplanted from

the West Coast to a suburban garden,
they raised their heads and flowers emerged
each spring to mark the passing seasons
as bulblets appeared in their world and ours.

Each time we upped and moved from one
place to the next, so did they, adapting
as we did to life's changing latitudes,
and now, in lockdown, we celebrate

more than fifty years together, marked not
with fanfares, parties or floral bouquets,
but with our gathering of glowing lachenalias
and their raised-up, mauve vuvuzelas.

Nightjar
~ for Sue

This evening, the song rolls out its full-throated notes
among the trees beside the river. A nightjar sings
the call we render as 'Good Lord, deliver us'.

The call delivers us the stone cottage on a farm
in Namaqualand where, brimful of sunshine
and spring flowers, we sat under tilting stars

while the nightjar tolled its six clear notes.
Now the sky above the river is charged with song,
echoing the call that rang out over the closed heads

of fields of daisies hiding their faces from the dark…
And we, listening again to the bird whose incantation
you heard there for the first time, echo its plea.

Good Lord, deliver us now, if you can, from the grief
of losing her to the darkness, her bright face closed,
revive her gentle spirit to sing and let us not

lose all to the silence where this call no longer reaches.

From Chipinda Pools

You made me promise to return
with a handful of poems
but I've only a sheaf of pictures
clutched in my mind
to offer you from
Chipinda Pools.

I would have liked to give you
a poem about the spruce fish eagle
and the gleam of his feathers
as he glides above the river
on an early foray into light,
let you hear him throw

the full echoing waves
of his downriver call,
watch him slice a path through streaming air,
hold it in his billowing wings,
then swoop and tear the river's skin,
spark flakes of light around his prey.

I'd like to show you, too,
the sun's probing fingers lift
from the palettes of mopane leaves
those shadow hues of violet and lemon
buffed beneath the strong browns and greens,
sculpt edges around lion tracks in the sand.

But these few pictures, strung together
with the sharp sweet sting of bushwillow blooms,
are all I can offer you
instead of the handful of poems
you asked me to bring to you
from Chipinda Pools.

Lost
~ Lake Kariba, December 2015

The *Sealion* quivered before it stopped.
Out went the ripples, shivering towards
a line of wavering mountain rims.
Then they died and once again
the lake's black mirror calm returned.

The few who'd wished to swim appeared
and in plunged four pale bodies.
Those who watched cheered as the lake
briefly swallowed them just before
they surfaced, laughing, and stroked away

from the boat as it hung above where birds
once called and flew through corridors
of air that led through winding valleys
and onto plains beyond the hills,
as it hung above the rusted scythes

and sunken fields, above the kraals
where cattle had once stood or slept,
where people walked about each day
while tending crops – lost below
cerulean acres of reflected sky.

Cold to the bone, they climbed on deck
to eyes that went on staring past
them at the depths, the blue-black depths
where Nyaminyami, the river god,
still waits with drowned ancestral graves.

Gleaning
~ *Bloubergstrand, 2021*

A mound of tangled kelp
huddles in the mass of empty
mussel shells on the beach.

Now a frond of kelp
gropes among the shells,
becomes an old man's sleeve.

Bent over, sifting, probing,
he picks an object up
and holds it to the light

to be inspected. It's a lump
of coal worn down to shine
by rolling on the floor of the sea

and washed up onto the sand
by last week's storm.
He drops it in his pail.

The man, too, is one
of those rolled around by life,
its calm days and its storms,

before being cast up here,
on his face a lineage clear
that stretches back to foragers

of centuries past who scoured
beaches for their sustenance,
forward to those others who

will go on combing along
this littoral for what's been left
when we've all gone elsewhere.

Beachings

On the small shelly beach,
where the whispering stream
still trickles down through reeds
to meet the holding sand
we watch them once again,
five sun-streaked little heads
above their beer-brown bodies
bent intently over their task:
with flying plastic spades
they coax the grumbling stream
to curl around and settle
behind their piled-up wall of sand
raised into a dam.

The tendrils of our memory
go back some thirty years,
to catch their parents
with sun-bleached fronds
flopping over their eyes,
thrusting tight-cupped hands
into sand to tame the same
recalcitrant stream and make
their miniature dam on the beach
while puffs of laughter
flitter around their tangled heads
like butterflies.

And burrowing further still,
we glimpse a group of bodies,
brown as lychee pips,

squatting on the beach.
Small fists grasp stone
scrapers and blades, prising open
the shellfish newly culled
at low tide from the rocks,
words clicking and sparking
as they scoop up water
in hollow ostrich eggs
from this same spluttering stream.

At the Waterhole
~ *Nossop, Kalahari*

From the hide, pale faces squint out into the light
and fix upon the pool where dark shapes coagulate;
a slope-shouldered brown hyena slinks down
to sip before oozing away in its shaggy pelt.

Jackals scurry after insects drawn by the light;
scorched wings fall like leaves to the ground.
Two bat-eared foxes, listening intently, circle near;
the jackals arch their backs and bristle their fur.

As darkness thickens, clicks punctuate the air,
stone cracking against stone, or bricks clinking.
The echolocation of airborne bats? But no,
a voice whispers, "It's barking geckoes!"

The way we walk back to our tents presents
us as we are: our heavy footfalls silencing
those who lived here many years before us,
whose clicking speech is echoed now in the Morse

code of fellow desert dwellers also near extinction.

The Fishermen on Fish Hoek Beach

in slow rhythmic pulls, drag
their half-moon net from the sea
and spill its slithery, silver haul out on
the sand. Webbed in the tangle of rope,
a crumpled shape with matted feathers
and open beak, head lolling, limp,
an albatross from far beyond
the steady pulse of shore-bound waves.

A knife flashes and slices open
the bulging belly. Sliding out,
not a mash of fish, but a garbage bin
of red plastic bottle tops,
tangled strands of yellow string
and nests of fishing line – omens
of our future, more telling than
tea leaves at the bottom of a cup.

Candelabra Lilies

Two strong stems, a hand span apart
grow parallel, but so close together
their branches are intertwined.

From the head of these two stems
spokes radiate, each cradling at its fingertips
a damask-pink, swaddled candle.

The air flows freely around the two
and from the giant dandelion heads
the branch tips slowly unfurl their buds,

then brightly flare their fiery blooms
to swell and glow more closely interlaced,
each giving the other light-boned support.

When dry, the candelabra flower heads
will roll across the wind-driven veld
like spinning catherine wheels, their circular

cages flinging their seeds across the land.
And we, our tumbling times now over,
our days of cartwheeling across the earth,

whirling at the whimsy of the wind,
hope that we too, now rooted close,
and holding still a hand span apart,

will ever give each other
the same airy buoyancy and support.

Sugarbush

On the path, the sun lights up and creams
the flower head of the sugarbush, cradling
its translucent cup in the lifting wind
while below, the upside-down,
ice-cream-cone buds are still closed.
Dry, pointed relics of last year's flowering
hold their seeds in tight brown fists
that wait for the fires of renewal.

"It's like a story," the child's voice pipes.
"The closed one is the beginning.
And there, look, the story gets going,
like that open flower, and ends
with that one there, closed and dead."
– And we, who clasp our dry brown fists
tightly around our hiking sticks,
find it easier now to face the flames

that fire renewal at our stories' end.

On Noordhoek Peak

> ...where the sun beats,
> And the dead tree gives no shelter, the cricket no relief,
> And the dry stone no sound of water.
> TS Eliot, *The Waste Land*

The fynbos droops in the heat.
The dogs sniff in vain for accustomed springs
or even muddy puddles on the trail
that leads up from the dam.
We flop down on the rocks at the peak,
haul out bottles of lukewarm water
for ourselves and the dogs.
Far below, the leaden air shimmers
over the sand of Hout Bay beach.

All is so quiet that suddenly we can hear it,
a little stream trickling somewhere
out from between the rocks
beyond and beneath our feet.
Standing and peering over the edge
for the miracle of water from bare rock
we see, not a latter-day Moses with his staff,
but rather a red-faced hiker
fumbling with his zip.

Absence
~ *Paris, 2015*

I'm now an amateur flâneur wandering
the streets of the Latin Quarter, my eyes
guzzling great towers of macaroons,
the pink, the green and the brown
chez les patisseries, but you aren't there.

My feet are drawn by the magnetism
of Notre Dame's jewelled windows.
Waves of music flood out of the great organ,
settling in quiet pools in secluded chapels
but no, I can't find you, you're not there.

Nor in the Louvre, where Michelangelo's
somnolent slaves struggle to emerge
from their marble blocks, not strolling
in the Jardin du Luxembourg, under
the raised fists of pollarded chestnut trees,

nor near Saint-Julien-le-Pauvre, at the arthritic
foot of the oldest locust tree in Paris,
where we used to meet after having visited
Shakespeare and Co. It's no good. No matter
where I search, you're not there, or anywhere.

Locks
~ Paris, 2015

Modern lovers don't carve
their initials in a heart pierced by
an arrow on a tree; instead,
these days, they hope for a more
metallic immortality.

Two locks are clamped together
and locked onto the railing of a bridge
above the Seine, hoping the locks
will keep their love forever meshed
on this grand arc over the Seine.

The keys are dropped into the flow.
On the far bank, the flying buttresses
that hold up Notre Dame wrap
in a cage of sacred stone the flight
of humans towards a love divine.

Chartres Revisited

Twin masts rise above the yellow sea of ripening wheat.
The vast nave anchored here is suffused with light –
red, blue and green, filtered through a stained-glass mosaic.
A solitary woman shuffles slowly along labyrinthine coils;
her head is bowed low and her eyes are squeezed shut.
Feet bare on cold stone, she follows the hallowed route,
her angled face kept closed to the wide world outside.

At the centre she halts, raising her eyes heavenwards,
then crosses herself, steeples her hands under her chin,
and turns. Crossing the threshold stone again, she
takes up her shoes and leaves under the glowing rose.
Our younger selves skip behind her, recalling Hopkins'
'Glory be to God for dappled things', the day tessellated
by morning light raining emeralds, sapphires and rubies.

Chameleon

In the labour ward, she recalls
the words of her friend:
"Being in labour's like trying to push
a rugby ball through a hosepipe."

In a haze of pain, she drifts
back to her childhood self,
when once with dangling limbs she lay
astraddle her favourite branch

in the old apricot tree,
watching a small creature
on the branch with her,
a tiny dragon in spiky green

battledress streaked with
dusty pink and grey, and splayed
hands and feet to grip the bark.
As she watched, the knobbly

creature pushed out a small
grey sausage, and then another,
until three little packages were lying
on the branch. One by one

they unfolded into perfect replicas
of their mother, who rolled her
marble eyes over each of them
before moving off in her

camouflage uniform.
When at last her own grey bundle
has been delivered to the ward,
she lets go and relaxes,

wondering whether or not
it too in time will uncurl
into a miniature replica of
its mother when she was a girl.

The Way Out

It seemed the best way out.
Why risk the whittled limbs,
the tremors and slammed doors,
the slanted stares, the drawing away?

And so, it was done…
Though nightly, at 10 or 2
and then at 6am again,
you hear it and you clutch your arms

around your chest and try
to rock yourself to sleep,
to deaden those cries
of the blighted child,
the baby stilled before being born.

Birthing

The nurse bustles in, glances at the taut face,
suggests pethidine. The beached shape on the bed
tenses, clenches her fists and shakes her head.
She wants no foreign substance to filter through
her blood to the life coiled inside kicking for release.

Her body cramps again; waves of pain rise
in a steady rhythm, higher and higher, swelling
to a sharp pinnacle. Her muscles are violin strings
pulled ever tauter, to splitting point. She gasps.
The fist squeezing her slowly relaxes its grip

so that she's surfing smoothly down from the crest
of pain to the other side, where a calm trough awaits.
But once again she's grabbed in a grip of steel.
It rises to its peak before a slithery bundle
is pushed out into waiting hands in a giant heave.

Fifteen years later, she watches him on his board
slicing through the waves, flying up, then surfing
down glassy slopes. In her belly she feels a tightening,
a cramping, that grips and then relaxes, releasing
the overflowing sense of joy she never forgets.

Out of Sync

The rasp that shreds the air
    on this forest fringe

shows that somewhere near
    lurks a dissonance:

a call at variance with its
    bearer's elegant dress.

Such cacophony signals
    presence among the leaves,

a sprightly bright green crest
    above wide-cocked eye

and flashes of red-hibiscus wings –
    and this unlikely mix

of emerald-and-ruby feathers
    and steel-wool syrinx

is the tree-top turaco, Knysna loerie
    in its flamenco best.

Courting

He thrusts his clutch of tulips in her face
and says, "I bought these beauties just for you,"
each stem standing stiffly in its place.

While she thinks of mountain walks, the place
of streams and pools, where disas bloom, the view,
he thrusts his clutch of tulips in her face.

Sharply pointed petals, armed for the chase
display their bright colours, to dazzle on cue
each stem standing stiffly in its place…

She loves buchu flowers, soft froth of lace
tumbling herbal scents; these scentless grew.
He thrusts his clutch of tulips in her face

but, hothouse nurtured, they can't displace
her fragrant fynbos – they're the wrong billet-doux
each stem standing stiffly in its place.

She doesn't welcome his persistent chase –
his flowers are not the right kind to woo –
but he thrusts his clutch of tulips in her face
each stem standing stiffly in its place.

Cancer Bush

A few rusty blooms still cling on
among the pale inflated seed capsules
hovering like ghosts of miniature canoes.

Leaning into her frailty, my niece stops
and relates how, as a child, she would
launch them to float dreamily downstream

until they met a rock or sunken log
that grabbed at the passing flotilla,
the eddies making them bob and swerve.

Some of the pods are still flecked with pink,
but most are bleached white, papery vessels
carrying the relics of a fruitful year.

She has plans to share with her young son
a launching of these craft once she has
grown stronger. But the rustling

of the dry husks whispers that the power
to heal held in their name is paper-thin.
For his sake, she can still bob and swerve,
keeping afloat the hope of them carrying on.

Corona Paranoia

Now, anything shaped like a globe
is suspect, it seems. Even pollen grains
under a microscope look sinister,

and the spiky head of a dandelion,
when probed, reveals a dark heart
in seeds sent flying with a single breath.

On the path, a pill millipede coils itself
like a pangolin, while the moon
wears a misty aura like a surgical mask.

Bristled sea urchins in rock pools
wield bright stilettos, and the centre
of a sunflower repels the onlooker,

Fibonacci's spiral with its encircling crown
of pointed sepals whirling us down
and into a dense black hole.

Walking between Walls

On our last hike before lockdown, we jaunt up
a mountain path, dogs dancing around our feet.
A sunbird on an erica flashes iridescence in green
and red, while all around us, fynbos sings.

A wall of sandstone curves round on one side
to hold us in its protective arc, while
in the bay far below, faint whispering waves
are floating their endless scribbles of foam.

Then everyone stops in mid-stride as from
a clump of bush a yellow gush erupts, rising
knee-high before steadying into a copper tube
that opens a hood with wide flanges spread.

Two black beads spark above a flickering tongue.
The snake flexes like an upraised arm. We grab
both dogs and back away as it quivers and sways
before pouring itself back into the ground.

On our way down, the path trembles under
our tread, the rock walls contract, closing in.
We feel expelled, descend, returning to pace
around the limits of our lockdown yards.

Mona Lisa

At eighty-nine, my mother sat
upright in bed and announced,
"I want to go, I've had enough.
I've had all I could from life."

But matron demurred and replied,
"I'm afraid you can't and must stay on,
and be grateful for the extra time
as God's not ready for you yet."

My mother gave a Mona Lisa smile.
"Ah," she said, "that's only because,
omniscient though She might be,
God doesn't know what She's missing."

Assisted Living

On my last visit, near the end,
I found my mother flushed, sitting up in bed.
The headlines on her lap shrieked

"Elderly woman killed in shark attack"
and "Red bathing cap found on beach".
"I'm sorry you saw that," I muttered.

She shook her head vehemently.
"Oh no, it's far better to go out with a splash,
doing what you love, than subside

slowly, meekly, into sinking sands
of old age and oblivion. Of course,
I can't get to the beach, so I'm

waiting for a new book I've ordered.
But meanwhile, on your next visit,
please bring me a red shower cap."

Afterwards, on her bedside table,
I found a new copy of a novel
by Zakes Mda, called *Ways of Dying*.

The Last Stretch

You led us over mountain peaks, sure-footed
as a klipspringer on the rocks, always stretched
a hand to steady our steps on the steep slopes
or ledges hanging high above the contour path.

February drew us up Skeleton Gorge
to the aqueduct, where you pointed out
red disas, gold-dusted butterflies flaring
silky wings in nests of moss above the stream.

In the Cederberg, we watched with you
as a silver moon briefly shredded
in the skeletal branches of a cedar tree
before slowly gliding across the sky.

Now, you clutch my arm as we walk
along the passage of the Sunshine Ward.
You've not eaten or spoken for days on end.
Your eyes have sunk deep into your head.

A window opposite shows a scrap of garden
where a bush holds a struggle of blue flowers.
You point at it and I open the window,
guiding your hand through the space.

Your fingers tremble as you stretch towards
a flower. Your face unfolds. "Ah, the same,
still so soft." You turn to me and I whisper,
"Plumbago." The name hovers on your lips
as we walk back on the stretch of lino.

Lagoon
~ Langebaan

As you swim in the turquoise lagoon
that stretches brimming from the shore
to far limestone hills, remember her.

Stitch her life into yours as you tack
across the shimmering sheet of moiré silk,
your arms like needles rising and diving.

Sense beside you the shadow of a presence
that moved in tandem with you from
your childhood through your adult days

before being cut adrift in throbbing pain.
She is no longer there to match you
stroke for stroke, but as you swim, imagine

bubbles swarming in a cloud of light
to encircle her. You sense, beyond the hills,
the way that suffering figure slipped off

its sheath of unremitting pain, the way
it folded, finally, into its last easeful sleep.
Do not drop the torch of that bright life
but hold it high to help illuminate your own.

The Hive

Just before you left for university,
your father cast a critical eye over your books.
No proper dictionary, he noted.
Later, he returned cradling the *Shorter Oxford*.

The price back then, fading now,
was about eight pounds.
Placed on the bathroom scale,
it weighed much the same.

Kept next to Chaucer, Shakespeare and Plato,
over the years it led you through
the hive of tantalising meanings,
intoxicating you with its rich mead.

But now, your fingers no longer leap
from page to page, tiptoeing instead
through the hive's long, winding passages
in search of just the right words to distil
a father's love.

Down, Not Out

An active sportsman all his life,
he strode into his eighties
claiming he was now well beyond
his allotted three-score years and ten,
so could enjoy copious draughts
of good red wine in his "injury time".

At 85, he was felled by a stroke.
He mumbled that it was "par for
the course". Flat on his back, he
resumed walking, raising and
stretching each leg until he could
hobble with his family along a path.

In Kirstenbosch, his two sticks stuttered
to a halt at the old yellowwood tree
lying prone on the grass. A sudden storm
had felled it and left it split in two.
His face crumpled to see the proud tower
laid low, but its limbs were brandishing

green flags, new growth rising in a tide
that swept over the prostrate form.
He stopped, stumbled towards the old tree
and, drawing his hand slowly across
the wrinkled bark and fresh leaves, said:
"If you can do it, old boy, so can I."

Courgettes

I think of you always when I'm cooking courgettes,
not when Goldberg variations ripple into the night.
Neither Dvořák nor Schubert quite do it for me;
not even Beethoven's late, great sublime quartets.

I don't think of you when I stare at False Bay,
or I'm watching grey otters tumbling in-out a gully.
Gannets spearing the sea can't quite do it for me,
or the sun flaring deep apricot just as it sets.

I don't stroke passing dachshunds, your favourite pets,
don't see paintings in rock pools as you used to do;
but you once said, "Don't cut them, it spoils their flavour,"
so I think of you always when I'm cooking courgettes.

In Dire Need

I never thought that I could be
In thrall to a mere hinge, a knee.
A knee whose foot was always pressed
On hiking trails or mountain crest.

A knee that would skip up hill, down dale
Fly over boulders, never quail
Up India Venster, down Left Face B –
Table Mountain a molehill for this devotee.

Now this knee shoots shafts of pain along my leg
Not bending, it buckles, it's a powder keg
About to blow up, sending splinters of bone
Showering over the fynbos all the way home.

I'm told that the fault is entirely mine
Caused by years of abuse to knees and to spine.
On Sundays, genuflecting with a lens before a flower,
I should have bent my knees, indoors, to a higher power!

Descending a Staircase

She descends the spiral staircase carefully,
lifting each foot, holding it poised
for a second before
placing it on the next step down.

He stands and watches from below,
smiling as she reaches his side.
"You descend so delicately," he says,
"like a graceful ballet dancer."

With a dicey knee, she sees instead
a chameleon lifting up one leg,
holding it poised before inching forward
and lowering it to the next inch of the branch.

Hospital Visit

The day they took my father to hospital
his dog, Retna, drooped his tail to half-mast,
crept away, curled into a foetal knot
and shuttered his eyes in his paws.

For five days, he hardly stirred, only
lifted his head to lap a little water,
but when we tried to coax him to eat,
he turned away from the proffered bowl.

On the sixth day, we helped my mother wrap him
in a blanket and sneak him into the ward.
His eyes flickered when he saw the inert form
lying like a funeral figure on a slab.

My father reached out a trembling hand
to pat his head. Retna stared into his face,
licked his hand, then lay down
on the floor beside the bed.

Someone spoke of cancer. That night,
we turned away from our plates, but Retna,
for the first time, put his nose into his bowl
and raised his flagpole tail to lift our hopes.

Visiting Hour

Strands of old man's beard clutch
onto a dry branch
in an earthenware pot placed
on the counter at reception.

Red lights flash around his bed,
while something hums in the background.
A plastic tube drains his stomach,
another drips morphine into his arm.

His voice is snagged on the tube stuck in
his throat; he talks in croaks
as digits rise and fall
impassively on the sentry screen.

Her hand holds his fluttering palm,
his eyes flitting between
hers and wind-whipped leaves that surge
beyond the window frame.

The clock winds down, she has to go.
Halfway down the stairs,
a picture of gannet beaks spiking up to spear
a solitary bird flying above their heads.

Carpe

He would pick strawberries with tender care,
holding each plump berry, caressing
it off the stalk, as if for fear
of the slightest bruising.

Gentled, too, each day as it came along,
subtly handling time with supple fingertips
'on song', relishing each moment
in rhyme with others,

like ripe fruit readily enjoyed
under a duvet of clotted cream,
carpe with care unspoken, and buoyed,
the last fruit to him would seem

to simply ease itself off the stalk.

Packing Up

The furniture was not so bad, although
the bed still held its furrowed dip,
a wavering line, curved round
at the top, like a centred question,
where you used to lie.

The desk, its clutter of pens and paper
tossed into boxes, bore hardly a trace.
The chest of drawers divested of your
clothes could be anyone's now,
the yellowwood glowing in autumnal sun.

Unyielding wooden surfaces cannot retain
the imprint of a human form;
it was easy to dispatch all that.
But then the books, the magic pages
you used to read out loud to us –

these books still hold the imprint of your fingers.
Sometimes you would linger on a phrase –
fingertips pressing to unfold a word, an idea –
those words still vibrate, still hold
the warm brown cadence of your voice.

Eclipse

On the lawn
the child, aged two, stares moon-eyed
at the drama in the night sky
where the well-loved silver face,
so often beaming down for his delight,

now, tonight,
has a creeping edge of blackness
as though blinds
pulled in slow motion were dragging
a circle of darkness up from below.

"Oh, no!" he cries. "The big dark
is eating up the moon's face."
He rushes inside, stops, then asks
about that empty chair –
"Where granpa gone?"

And later, when I turn heavy eyes
to your face on the white slab of the hospital bed,
his words scatter like dried petals
across your still form
as the big dark keeps gnawing
at the pale orb of your face.

October Lilies
(Bonatea speciosa)
~ for my father (1910–2003)

Despite the passing tally of seasons,
every year the whorls of green
rise from black earth. Their glossy leaves
pirouette and reach up for the clouds.

Later on, the stalks will start to froth
their spikes of frilled white petals under
emerald bonnets – the lacy blossoms
of green wood orchids that you loved.

But now, the glossy sceptres stand without
the fountains of their creamy flowers,
waiting for October, your birthday month,
not yet marked for us on granite grey

but by these bursts of efflorescence
lighting up like torches all the paths
we used to walk with you through
wind-clipped, leaning coastal bush.

Grave Matters
~ *Churchhaven graveyard*

On long yellow legs
he high-steps between slabs
of lichen-feathered remembrance.
Browns, beige and soft greys colour
this dikkop's granite world.

Gazing past the church
towards the lagoon, he spots
intruders, then freezes,
fixing a sharp yellow eye
on the glint of binoculars.

He flashes black flight feathers
in menace, then flies off
cranking his curse
in mournful falling pitch:
"You will soon be down

among these, and bear
my curse forever if you dare
to even think of me
as a spotted thick-knee."

Paternoster

A weekend in lockdown takes us up the coast
to Paternoster, among ebullient spring flowers:
bright daisies and delicate towers
of mauve lachenalias pointing to the sky.

Then on to Velddrif for bokkoms and a favourite
fish restaurant on the river. But no bokkoms
are hanging out to dry on the bank or in the sheds
and the rustic shell of Die Vishuis is shuttered and locked.

No 'fish of the day' chalked up on the blackboard
at the dark door. Instead, blue lettering
spells out the obituary:
Hierdie klein juweel het gesterf op 30/06/21.

A small epigraph below states "Life lessons".
Is 'lessons' noun or verb? Either way,
it spells out what life teaches: it lessens,
until the point where no paternosters

can ward off the demise.

Childhood

Childhood rides bareback through the veld
on a palomino, or along a farm track,
galloping across fields of ruminating cows;

stops to converse with a passing bushbuck;
waves to a soaring black eagle overhead;
sleeps at last in a safe, warm bed.

But childhood can also have an Uncle Arthur,
a friend of the family, unmarried, who comes
to visit on Wednesdays, for a family meal;

gives children lavish gifts, enjoys games,
the boisterous ones especially. Until the day
she sees handprints on her brother's buttocks.

"It's nothing," he stammers, "just a game
I play with Uncle Arthur after school, at his flat.
It's our secret." Her father's eyes flash. Uncle Arthur
never comes to visit on a Wednesday again.

Gnarling

As they tread their usual path
along the riverbank, their feet
stumble on gnarled roots
of the ancient umbrella pines.

He curses; she shivers, thinks
that as they enter their final stretch
he is becoming snappy,
crocodile-skinned.

Like the gnarling roots
of the old pines, what should be
underground now pushes up
to the surface in thick, twisted ropes

with knobbly protrusions thrust up
like eyeballs to see what kind of life
they are supporting, inadvertently
tripping up unwary feet.

A Letter to Stalin's Daughter
~ *April 2022*

What would you say today, Svetlana,
you whose childhood was whittled away,
slash by slash, by a blade of steel
wielded by an unknown hand,
as aunts, cousins, family friends
were scythed away?

What did you think, Svetlana,
when the truth slapped against you
and you, the princess, had to live on
in the monster's den, knowing
your mother had made herself
disappear before the steel struck?

And what would you feel now, Svetlana,
seeing rows of prams holding cupped
nests to clasp those fledglings fleeing
from their blasted homes, while
other families creep underground
like moles, no food, water or sun?

What would you say to your father's
reincarnation, you who foresaw
that he would drive Russia
through rivers of blood, you who
fled from the hellhole to find
a freer world, what to say

to the flood of new refugees driven
from their homes, what could you say,
Svetlana, in any of your languages –
Russian, French, German, English –
when words are forged on an anvil of lies
shapeshifting in the service of an ersatz czar?

Doll's House

An old man crawls through black smoke,
dodging splintered tables and chairs.
The front of his apartment block
has seemingly been ripped right off,
exposing all the furniture of smashed lives.
Pictures lie broken, shedding shards of glass.

The TV screen briefly flickers and dies.
A childhood memory flashes into mind
of a miniature double-storey house,
its tiny front door ready to open
wide in welcome, with fleeting glimpses
of rooms and busy little people,

and if ever you swung the façade open,
you could walk your fingers through
the perfect interior – entrance hall,
a dining room with table and chairs,
upstairs, one bedroom with a double bed,
another with two singles, a bathroom.

Downstairs, in the kitchen, our favourite:
a kettle stands ready with water for tea.
A china tea set is waiting next to it
for the Lilliputian people – father in suit,
mother in floral dress, with a perky
white dog sitting beside two little children.

The memory fades and the screen comes
back into focus to reveal the old man
clawing his way to a shattered desk
surrounded by papers blasted out.
He sifts through the mess, searching
for… what? A passport? An ID?

Photographs that he can take with him to
another life? The shredded curtains
flutter in the wind. Explosions continue
to sound elsewhere. He moves to
a blackened kitchen in search of the kettle.
It's gone, blown into the street below.

Ginkgo
~ *Kirstenbosch*

This sentinel stands on the vantage point
that overlooks the Dell, shepherding the green
flocks of spiky cycads laid out around its feet,
fellow travellers from the distant Jurassic.

In autumn, its twin-lobed golden hearts
pump sunshine back at the sky before
l'arbre aux écus sheds bright golden coins
to pave all the ground in the surround.

Temple trees, they survived for hundreds
of years clustered around Buddhist temples
in China, until gangs of communist zealots
arrived and torched the great monasteries.

Like a phoenix in summer, it spurts feathery
fountains from layered branches held wide,
as if in welcome. In winter, a skeletal tree of life,
it holds deep in its memory the mushroom

cloud that on a clear August day consumed
the heart of Hiroshima, a few ginkgoes
the only living survivors left standing
anywhere near the middle of the fiery core.

When Does Time Bring Relief?

When does time start bringing relief?
Not when leaves dressed at last
in yellow-and-russet motley lose
their grip and fall to meet the loam.
Not when clouds of white terns wheel,

then lift off northwards leaving us
with nearly empty skies, nor when
the curlew sandpiper's pale underparts
start to flush warm chestnut for
migration to distant ends of the world.

How to measure time – in days or weeks
or years? – when it comes rippling out
in circles from the black hole dropped
into the centre of our lives to spread
between the present and distant shores?

The Purple Season
~ *Kirstenbosch, 2023*

The purple season has come.
Mauve spikes are sprouting from
the crown of the umzimbeet.

The deep murmur of carpenter bees
lumbering from bloom to bloom
as they mine the golden pollen

vibrates the charged air around
the bright yellows, whites and oranges
of spring and summer

now fading steadily to make way
for the more sombre hues
of the rainbow's violet end.

Red disas and crimson crassula
preen themselves to lure
a hovering mountain pride butterfly…

but the mountain's too high for us now
and I must take your arm
as with faltering steps we pass

the buoyant, love-flower globes
of blue agapanthus pointing
distilled-sky trumpets at the clouds

and head in silence to the purple ones
that mark a different kind of season,
their aubergine fingers pointing down.

After

After a sad season's absence,
the swallows sweep back, homing
in on their old roosting place
in the reeds beside the river.

They bear no trace of that spell
underground that Aristotle
believed they had to endure
during sombre winter.

We, who long to surface
after a joyless season submerged
like Persephone in funereal gloom,
fly with Aristotle's swallows

as they swoop in droves over
the lawn, scooping up insects
now emerging after the rain.
We skim with them in spirit

over the newly green expanse
that flows down to the river
as circling back and forth
they sweep up the detritus

of the buried year

Spotted Eagle Owls
~ *Kirstenbosch*

For years, they nested in a hollow
among rocks at the base of a wild peach tree
where several paths converge.

Visitors would stop to stare at the tufted faces
in the makeshift nest, some thrusting
long lenses into their personal space.

To escape the paparazzi, they moved
to a lush planter in the paved forecourt.
Weeks passed, then two tiny white fluffballs

peeped out from under their grey duvet
to peer at the fish in the pond below.
Later, they stretched their spiky wings

in preparation for flight.
One must have tried too soon.
No camera caught the plunge into the pool.

Autumnal

The glowing cowl cupping the crest of the hill
deepens to blood-orange flame
as knob thorn and marula, drained of green,
black skeletons with skinny fingers,

stitch together earth and sky. Pools
in the riverbed lasso in silver the fading light,
stepping stones for the passage overhead
of the swelling mango moon.

Sky spaces that flicker in summer with bee-eaters,
blowtorch blue of kingfishers, and raptors
riding on thermals, are now voids
as migrants follow their compass needle north.

Yet the purple-crested loerie brightens the sky
for those of us still earthbound here
in the south, as it flashes a sudden flypast
in a blaze of poinsettia wings.

May the southern spring welcome the migrants'
return before we, too, set off on our own final
migration, north or further south, drawn
to that polar destination still unknown.

Message

What's the message of a poem?
they ask. Can we use it as a key
to unlock the mystery
of life?

A poem, you reply, one hopes,
held up to the light can be
a prism through which to see
another life.

The keyhole's just for peeping
at its small, fragile shelter
away from the welter
of life.

The Last Supper

In his house at Cloux, near Amboise
on the river Loire, an old man sits
at his table, writing intently.

This, the last page of one of Leonardo's
final works, on geometrical calculations,
ends abruptly.

It looks like an unfinished theorem,
the text breaking off in mid-sentence
with a flat "et cetera"

written after he'd heard a voice calling –
not the voice of his patron, François I,
nor the voice of his muse

with some mystical revelation,
some ultimate truth, but
the simple voice of mundane humanity,

the voice of his cook in the kitchen
summoning him from his work
"…because the soup is getting cold."

BIOGRAPHICAL NOTE
....

Adré Marshall taught English at various universities, most recently UCT. Her poetry has been published in numerous anthologies and journals, she has read at the McGregor Poetry Festival and is the author of a book on Henry James. Her translations from French into English include *Le Grand Livre de la Mémoire* and a book of critical commentary/articles for the Picasso and Africa exhibition at the Iziko South African National Gallery in Cape Town. One of her poems was placed 3rd in the 2022 AVBOB Poetry Competition, while another was shortlisted for the National Poetry Prize in 2023.

www.ingramcontent.com/pod-product-compliance
Lightning Source LLC
Chambersburg PA
CBHW050918160426
43194CB00011B/2459